Ring-Tail Possums

By Carmel Reilly

Contents

Possums in Town   2

Possum Food   4

Night Animals   7

A Possum Family   9

Possums Are Not Pets   12

Possums in Town

Ring-tail possums get their name from their curled tail.

The tail has a white tip.

fur

claws

curled tail

Some ring-tail possums
live in forests, but many
live in towns.

Possum Food

Ring-tail possums like to have a supply of leaves to eat.

But they eat other things, too.

Ring-tail possums like to eat blooms and fruit.

This possum stole some fruit from a garden!

Possums will even eat lemon peel or cactus!

A possum ate the lemon peel.

Night Animals

Ring-tail possums do a lot at night.

While people sleep, possums go out and play.

Sometimes they fight, too.

They jump from tree to tree and run on wires.

Their tails can help support them.

A Possum Family

Ring-tail possums live
in family groups.

Possum family groups live
in nests up in trees.

possum nest

A baby possum is a joey.

A ring-tail possum mother
can have two joeys
at a time.

possum joey

At first, the joey lives in
the mother possum's pouch.

But when it gets too big,
it rides on its mum's back.

Possums Are Not Pets

Ring-tailed possums are very cute, but they are wild animals.

Do not pat them, or you could get a painful nip!

Ring-tailed possums should not be kept as pets.

But you can see them in your yard when it's dark!

CHECKING FOR MEANING

1. Why are the possums in this text called ring-tail possums? *(Literal)*

2. What do possums eat? *(Literal)*

3. Why do you think possums live up in nests in the trees? *(Inferential)*

EXTENDING VOCABULARY

supply	What is a *supply* of gum leaves? What are other words that mean the same as *supply*? E.g. quantity, amount, store.
sometimes	Look at the word *sometimes*. Explain that this is a compound word. Compound words are made by joining two or more smaller words to make a new word with a new meaning. What other compound words can you think of? E.g. breakfast, popcorn.
support	How does a possum's tail help support it? What do possums do with their tails to get support?

MOVING BEYOND THE TEXT

1. Why do you think possums have sharp claws?

2. What do we call animals that are more active at night than in the day? Introduce the term *nocturnal.* What other animals do you know that are awake at night-time?

3. Which other animals have a pouch for their babies? What are these pouched animals called? Introduce or revise the term *marsupials.*

4. What are some other animals that can't be kept as pets? Why is this?

THE SCHWA

a	e	i	o	u

PRACTICE WORDS

possums

a

forests

supply

garden

even

lemon

cactus

support

family

the

animals

painful

Possums

A

Family

The

possum

Possum

possum's